To the children and families who have shared their stories and experiences with me.

Library of Congress Cataloging – in – Publication Data

contents

to parents

How to use this book:

This book primarily addresses the basics of prevention and assertiveness for children ages 3 to 12 years old. It is a way to help you start the conversation on child abuse prevention. It is structured as an introductory book to give you the basic tools to prevent child sexual abuse or inappropriate touching.

The book is written using the female pronoun to facilitate the writing process. However, the concepts in the book are applicable to both girls and boys.

Review the book with your child every three months while role playing and giving your child opportunities to ask you questions. Child development researchers have documented that children need to practice their assertiveness skills in order to be able to use these skills when they need to. You will also discover that your child will ask you more advanced questions about her general sexual development as she grows older.

Three main goals for communicating with your child:

• Teach your child the concept of "private zones" and what parts of the body are considered private.

• Teach your child to recognize uncomfortable touches and assertive skills to end an uncomfortable situation.
• Teach your child not to keep secrets and to report anything that makes her uncomfortable to a trusted adult until the adult acts on her concern.

Furthermore, it is important to note that a child's understanding of complex concepts increases as her cognitive development matures. Most children will not understand abstract concepts until they are around 7 years old. (1)

Other good times to review this information are: each time your child starts a new activity, such as going to summer camp; before allowing your child to go for a sleep over; and whenever there is an incident of inappropriate touching in school, such as child-to-child private parts, even if your child was not directly involved.

Remember that a child does not understand that another young adult's or adult's intentions might be bad. Children have difficulty understanding that an adult's authority is not absolute. These two concepts are very abstract for children to grasp. Therefore, they need reinforcement throughout their developmental years.

laying the groundwork

When parents talk about child sexual abuse or inappropriate touching, they voice some of their greatest fears and concerns. As a parent, your apprehension is well justified, as child abuse statistics are grim. It is estimated that 1 in 3 girls and 1 in 7 boys will experience child sexual abuse ranging from unwanted touching to rape before the age of 18 years. (2, 3)

As a result, a prevention strategy that provides children with age-appropriate information, awareness skills, self-confidence, and support to protect themselves is imperative. Parents are a child's first teacher and the best people to start conversations about sexual development and child sexual abuse prevention. These conversations with children educate them about protecting their bodies, their innocence, and their minds and need to happen early on in their lives, continuing until they truly understand it. Otherwise, we risk the education they'll receive coming from a potential perpetrator, who will tell them that the unwanted touch they might receive is "their secret."

An effective prevention program requires parents to also have a positive guidance approach to parenting, which allows your child to develop the feelings of competence she needs to assertively know that her body is hers to protect and care for.

A positive guidance approach also helps the child know that conflicts can be resolved without hitting, that her body is to be respected, and nobody has the right to harm it or touch it in an unwanted way.

Creating body self-awareness and the vocabulary of prevention takes time and dedication by discussing the information in many ways, and reinforcing it using different tools. For a child, abstract concepts, such as understanding another's intention, will take time, eventually becoming clearer as child cognitive development matures.

She'll be able to understand a little bit around age three, when the discussion about body safety needs to start, and will understand much more in just six months.

With children, actions speak louder than words. When we create a safe environment for children, we allow them to explore, make mistakes, and, above all, come to us knowing that we will be there for them.

Creating a safe environment for your child to communicate with you is also very important.

Your child needs to feel that she can always go to you for help. So, in order to effectively prevent child abuse as a parent, we have to work on building an open, two-way communication system, letting your child tell her story. Practice letting your child tell her adventures without interruptions from

laying the groundwork

beginning to end.
Children need practice talking about themselves. When your child is telling you her adventures, listen to her and practice praising her. Those valuable, praising words are key to helping your child build her self-esteem and confidence. Continual interruptions and criticism shut the door to communications.

Finally, remember that as parents, every time we are faced with everyday challenges, such as getting your child to listen to you or getting your child to clean up, you have an opportunity to teach your child many important lessons. These lessons go beyond getting your child to clean up her toys. The way you communicate to your child lets her know that her feelings are respected, her time is respected, and her needs are met.

If you find yourself getting frustrated over your child's behavior, it helps to remember that the way you talk to her will teach her how to manage stress, communicate respectfully, handle conflict considering other people's feelings, and accomplish resolution without harming the other person emotionally.

Each time you get frustrated, think about it as an opportunity to be a role model for your child, she'll learn that she can always go to you for help without fearing being made fun of or being physically harmed.

Communicate Acceptance:

When your child knows that you love her and accept her just as she is, she'll develop a healthy self-image and self-esteem. If your child feels accepted, she is more likely to share her own difficulties, feelings, and problems with you.

This concept is expressed in words as much as in actions. Each time that you allow your child to kiss, hug, or decline a friendly hug or kiss from someone (even someone they are close to), she learns that her feelings are important and her body truly belongs to her.

During holiday times, when either bunny photos or Santa photos are popular among families, I see little kids forced to sit on unknown laps with the parents overriding the children's feelings. Forcing your child to sit on Santa's lap is detrimental for your child's self-confidence.

If your child does not want to sit on a stranger's lap, reinforce the message that it is okay to say no because your body belongs to you. Let your child know that it is also okay to not want a kiss or hug, even if your child knows the person and you are close to that person. While parents are concerned about "stranger danger," the reality is that 93% of the time, children are sexually abused or molested by someone they know and trust, such as a coach, an uncle, or a cousin. While some threat, albeit small,

laying the groundwork

might be attributed to strangers, the greater risk comes from familiar adults that the child knows. (4)

Example:

Danny says, "Mommy, I'm scared to sit on Santa's lap." Which response communicates acceptance and the message that your body belongs to you?

a- You're acting like a big baby! You know there's nothing to be scared of! It is just Santa.

b- I can see that you are frightened. You can choose to take the picture next to Santa, or we can just do a different family activity to commemorate the holiday.

Answer "b" communicates acceptance; it also coveys the message that your body belongs to you.

Give yourself permission to teach the assertiveness your child needs to protect herself. Encourage your child to say no if they dislike the tickling, kisses, or hugs. Give them permission and respect their decisions since their bodies belong to them.

Tips for Parents:

As your child grows older and starts to assert her individualism and her likes and dislikes, you can help her in this process by providing at least two choices of clothing

for the child to choose from, a variety of play toys, family activities, etc

A typical struggle with children comes when they refuse to wear what their parents want or refuse to eat what their parents want.

It is important that your child learns that she can choose and make decisions for herself. It will boost her self-esteem. Children are usually fine if they are offered two choices. For example, arrange two outfits for your child to pick from. She'll be happy to assert her self-determination, and at the same time, you'll avoid a struggle by having to force her to wear what you want.

Talking With Your Children Effectively:

Using correct anatomical terms for children's genitals is extremely important. A child needs to know that they have a vagina or a penis. Practice in front of the mirror until you get comfortable talking about these anatomical body parts without blushing.

If you teach your daughter to call her vagina "flower," she won't have the correct vocabulary to express an incident to a teacher or another adult. It is common for small children ages 4 and 5 to want to explore their body parts, and they might want to touch a classmate's private parts.

While this curiosity is developmentally appropriate, parents and teachers need to work on teaching children body boundaries.

This process is facilitated if a child reports to the teacher, "Mary just touched my vagina," rather than saying, "Mary touched my flower." In the second case, the teacher might dismiss the complaint as unimportant, making the child feel as if her problem is insignificant.

Teach your child that their vagina, penis, and bottom are their private parts using the correct anatomical terms.

Convey to your child the rules about other people not touching their private parts. Be as clear as possible and explain to her that when she was little, Mommy changed her diapers. Let your child know that as an older girl, she now can clean herself after using the bathroom. Teach your child to clean herself from an early age.

It is also important to talk to your child about the exceptions, such as going to the doctor. Let your child know that you will be with her during these exceptions.

If your child is in a daycare, learn about the daycare's policies about cleaning a child after using the bathroom. If your little one is still learning how to clean her bottom, you might want to discuss this with your daycare provider and come up with a plan that you also discuss with your child.

Take responsibility as a protective adult:

If your child is having play dates, learn about who is in the house. Have a conversation with your child and the other adult in the house about letting you know immediately if somebody else arrives unexpectedly. While you can educate your child, she is little and needs protection. (5)

Always have at least one designated adult that your child knows to go to, to let that person know if something does not feel right or feels uncomfortable.

Finally, work on taking away the stigma by talking on a daily basis with your child about body integrity. Your body is your own; you ask people before you touch. We don't touch others' private parts. Teach them general body boundaries.

6 myths about child sexual abuse prevention

Myth 1: It will have a negative impact on my child.

The work that this book encourages you to do with your child in terms of child sexual abuse prevention will not have any negative consequences. However, you are encouraged to seek additional help in case you feel that you need to know more about how to talk to your child before starting the conversation.

Myth 2: It can wait until she is older and able to understand better.

You can help your child develop a basic concept of knowing her private parts as early as 2.5 years old. Eventually, it will make sense to her.

Myth 3: Sexual abuse only happens to a certain economic group or race.

Child sexual abuse can happen to any child, regardless of her economic status or race.

Myth 4: Children know too much about sex.

Knowing about sex and prevention of child sexual abuse are two different things. Little children who are molested usually do not know about what is happening to them, and the situation is very confusing. In addition, it is always better for children to learn about sexual development and child sexual abuse prevention from their parents or an educated adult rather than learning about it from YouTube, older brothers, or older family friends, such as cousins.

Myth 5: Not talking about sexual abuse is a prevention strategy.

Many parents remember their own sexual development education and abuse prevention as nonexistent. In most homes, child sexual abuse was an off subject. Unfortunately, not talking about sexual development and child sexual abuse will not protect your child from being a victim.

Myth 6: Children know how to say no.

While most children know how to say no in everyday situations, they need to practice saying no in situations that involve unwanted touches. The research shows that under threats from an adult, most children feel overpowered and do not report the abuse, making the child just too frightened to protect herself. (6)

Note:

There is no right or wrong way to use this book to help your child learn healthy boundaries, just remain patient and respectful of your child's learning process.

Sincerely,

Jusleine Daniel, LCSW.

Writer's Note: This publication is designed to provide accurate and authoritative information in regard to the subject matter covered. It is provided with the understanding that if professional expert assistance or counseling is needed, the reader should seek the services of a competent professional counselor or social worker.

bibliography

Bibliography:

1 Pereda, Noemí, et al. "The Prevalence of Child Sexual Abuse in Community and Student Samples: A Meta-analysis." Clinical Psychology Review 29.4 (2009): 328-338.

2 Stoltenborgh, Marije, et al. "A Global Perspective on Child Sexual Abuse: Meta-analysis of Prevalence Around the World." Child Maltreatment 16.2 (2011): 79-101.

3 Finkelhor, David. "The Prevention of Childhood Sexual Abuse." The Future of Children 19.2 (2009): 169-194.

4 Walsh, Kerryann, and Leisa Brandon. "Their Children's First Educators: Parents' Views About Child Sexual Abuse Prevention Education." Journal of Child and Family Studies 21.5 (2012): 734-746.

Mabry, Malerie, and Navaz Peshotan Bhavnagri. "Perspective Taking of Immigrant Children: Utilizing Children's Literature and Related Activities."Multicultural Education 19.3 (2012): 48-54

5 Mabry, Malerie, and Navaz Peshotan Bhavnagri. "Perspective Taking of Immigrant Children: Utilizing Children's Literature and Related Activities."Multicultural Education 19.3 (2012): 48-54.

6 Barron, Ian G., and Keith J. Topping. "Survivor Experience of a Child Sexual Abuse Prevention Program a Pilot Study." Journal of interpersonal violence28.14 (2013): 2797-2812.

body safety coloring and activity book

Dear kids,

This book was written to help you to learn about how to protect your body and to practice your assertiveness skills by saying "no" if you dislike a certain touch. Even if the situation involves refusing a kiss from your aunt visiting from New York. You have the right to say no to her kiss! Isn't that great?

As you grow older, you might have more complicated questions about keeping your body safe. Always ask, since by asking you can learn important lessons about living a healthy and happy life!

Love,

Jusleine.

add color!

my body is mine to care for

I care for my body by eating healthy foods.

I care for my body when I exercise.

I care for my body when I rest.

I care for my body, and my body is mine to care for.

add color!

i love my body

I love my body, and I respect it.

I decide what to wear.

I decide what shoes to wear.

I care for my body, and my body is mine to care for.

add color!

i protect my body

I protect my body and my private zones.

When I go swimming, I cover my private zones.

When I go to the beach, I also cover my private zones.

I care for my body, and my body is mine to care for.

add color!

i can say yes

I love my family and my friends.

Sometimes I like to get hugs...

add color!

i can say no

...and sometimes I don't.

and this is ok. I can always say NO!

add color!

i can say si

Sometimes I like to get kisses...

add color!

i can say no

...and sometimes I don't.

And this is okay, too.

I care for my body, and my body is mine to care for.

add color!

i can say no

I can say no.

If somebody gives me a hug and I don't want it,

I can say no if I don't like how it feels.

If somebody gives me a kiss and I don't want it,

I can say no if I don't like how it feels.

add color!

touches that feel right

Touches that feel right.

Some touches make you feel warm and safe, and they feel just right.

Parents; use this space to draw pictures with your child depicting safe and warm touches. You can also take pictures of your child and yourself and glue them here.

touches that don't feel right

Touches that don't feel right.

Some touches make you feel angry, scared, or mixed up with worry and uncomfortable feelings. Some touches just feel bad.

I can say no if the touch makes me feel angry and scared.

I can tell _____ if somebody touches me in a way that makes me feel uncomfortable.

I can also tell _____ because I know they'll help me to feel safe.

add color!

what happens at the doctor's office?

What happens at the doctor's office?.

A doctor or nurse might touch my private parts during a checkup.

But my_____ goes to the doctor with me so that I know this is safe.

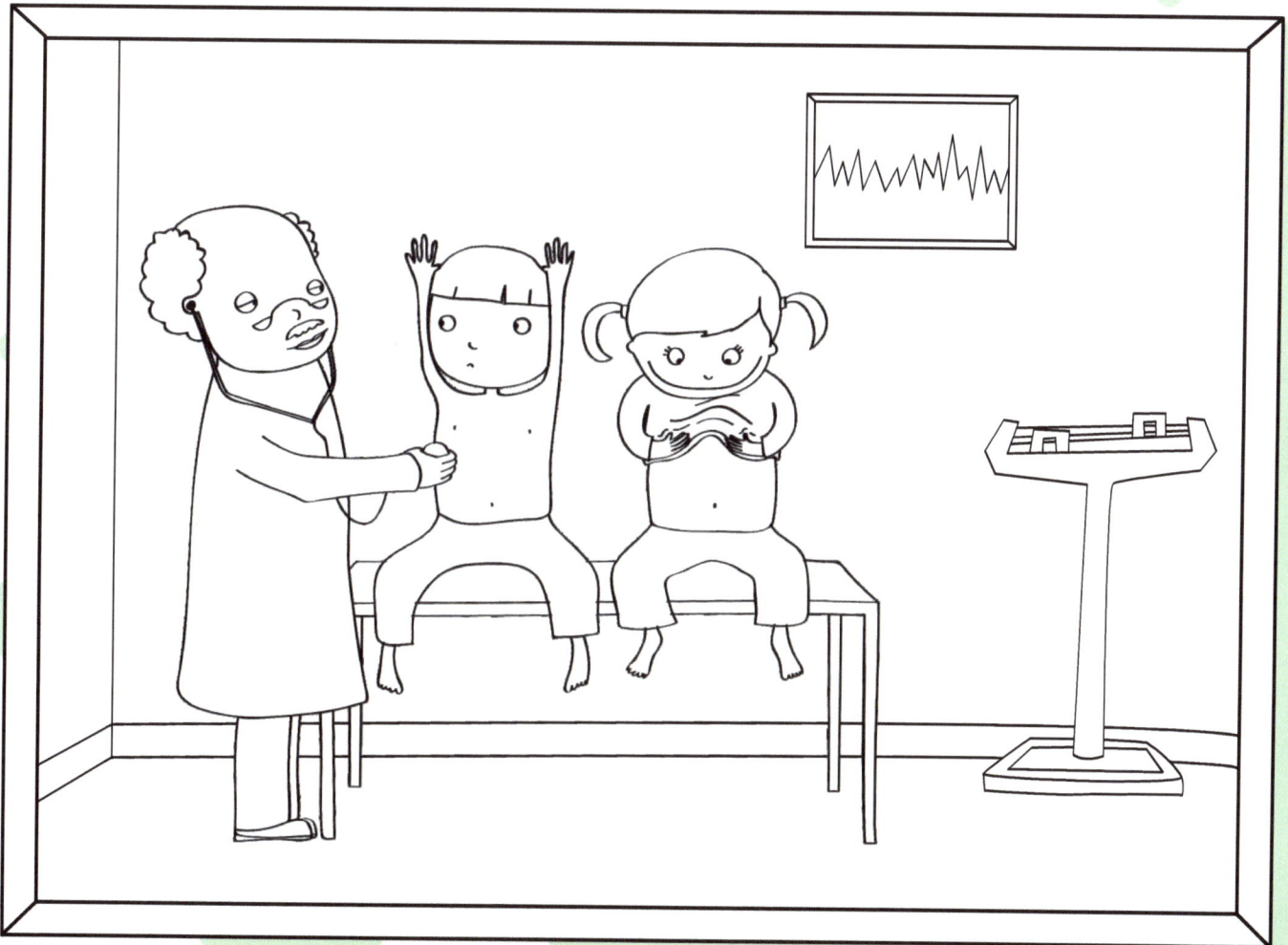

add color!

i protect my private parts

I protect my private parts

I know that nobody else touches my private parts. I know that even someone I know and love is not allowed to touch my private parts.

I also know not to keep secrets!

I take good care of my body, and I say no to touches that make me upset or scared.

add color!

i protect my private parts

I don't do anything that makes me feel uncomfortable.

I say no if someone asks me to touch or look at my private parts.

I say no if someone asks me to look at or touch his private parts.

I say no if someone asks me to look at or touch her private parts.

I say no if someone asks me to take off my clothes and not tell anybody.

I don't do anything that makes me feel **un·com·fort·a·ble.**

I can say, "No, don't touch me."

I can also _____ .

add color!

i protect my private parts

After saying no, I can get away from the person and tell my mom or dad.

I can also tell my teacher.

I can tell the school nurse.

add color!

i protect my private parts

I can tell a police officer.

Who else I can tell?_____ .

I keep on telling until a trusted adult listens to me.

I always trust my intuition!

add color!

space for drawing!

The end of the book and the beginning of a lifetime of caring for my body! Use this space to draw or paste pictures of the many ways in which you care for your body.

questions and comments

We welcome your questions and comments. Please email us to let us know your suggestions, questions, and how we can better help to have a greater impact in our child sexual abuse prevention efforts.

Contact us at creativolearning.jd@gmail.com.

If you'd like to contact Jusleine, please email her at creativolearning.jd@gmail.com.

Cover Designer: Keila La Rosa is a graphic designer and the art director for an advertising agency in Argentina. She enjoys riding her horse and mountain climbing with friends.

If you'd like to contact Keila, please email her at keilalarosa@gmail.com

We hope you enjoyed this Creativo Learning book!
www.creativolearning.com